# Hey Girls!
# Suspicious Guys
## You Should Be Extremely Wary Of...

Copyright 2009 By Tara Caplan

ALL RIGHTS RESERVED

No part of this book may be reproduced in any form without written permission by Tara Caplan.

ISBN 978-0578-03295-5

Published by Tara Caplan
Printed by Lulu Publishing

www.lulu.com

tarakcaplan@yahoo.com

http://www.myspace.com/suspiciousguys

http://www.facebook.com/caplan.comics

Hey Girls!
# Suspicious Guys
You Should Be Extremely Wary Of...

By Tara Caplan

Lulu Publishing

# Acknowledgements

I would like to thank my Dad, for introducing me to the highly entertaining world of comic books. I have many fond memories of the times we spent reading them together. So many thanks to my brother, Chris, for providing me with technical support, anytime I asked. Thank you, Mom, for always being so encouraging. Special thanks to Susan Joice, for sharing your design knowledge with me, and pointing me in the right direction. I am so thankful for all my friends, and fans, for making me feel so loved. And last, but certainly not least, I would like to give tremendous thanks to all the characters out there who inspire me to make comics!

# Introduction

***Hey Girls!* Suspicious Guys You Should Be Extremely Wary Of...** is a book comprised of sixty-six original characters from my comic zines of the same name, which I have been printing and selling since 2003 (see opposite page).

Though you may think you recognize an acquaintance, ex-boyfriend, neighbor, or that creepy guy who was hitting on you yesterday, all of my characters are fictional, based on the types of guys everyone seems to know.

Male humans have always fascinated me, with their strange, and often questionable courtship rituals, which led to my need to capture them in comic form.

Touchy-feely, 20-something "massage therapists"

"Just relax."

!

Pierced Fire Dancer Guys with overly embellished goatees.

# Cowboy Ravers

Guys who vainly preen their long blond hair.

Guys who display a perpetual, nervous grimace.

Drummer boys who openly proclaim that they are shamans.

Guys at parties who spend most of the time leaning cooly against a wall and half smiling lecherously at all the chicks.

Vacant-eyed, cult-vegetarians who always remember your name and want to know where you live.

Bar rats with mullets who constantly laugh at their own indecipherable attempts at humour.

Graying British "photographers" who invite you to their studio for some private sessions.

Guys who wear Renaissance clothes all year round.

"Good day, me lady!"

Streetside musicians wearing fantastical bird masks who try to seduce you with soulful, earnest, gazes, and jaunty, Celtic, melodies.

Zen, enlightened, white guys who tempt you with soft, peaceful gazes while savoring Maté from a gourd.

Little rat guys who try to charm you with flowery compliments and subtle invitations.

Guys who resemble a walking police sketch.

Guys that you witness getting freaky and primal late at night.

Deep, sensitive, brooding "artist" types who want to show you their sketchbook.

Guys who try to seduce the ladies by oiling themselves up like roasted chickens and squeezing into leopard print speedos.

Guys at parties who drunkenly undress you with their eyes as they fill up their plastic cup for the twelfth time.

"You from arown' here?"

Middle aged coffee shop trolls who you notice sketching you, composing a poem in your honor, or trying to gaze deeply into your soul.

Alpha-male duos who lure you in with Keystone and awesome keg stands.

Boozy businessmen with bedroom eyes and greasy comb-overs.

"Maybe we could get to know each other better on my yacht..."

Guys you meet in the park who have a guitar strapped to their back and are very high.

"Mmmm... You remind me... of a song, just a little tune I wrote, the other day..."

Young roosters who strut around rubbing their abs while throwing around desperate, sultry, lazy-eyed looks.

Guys with enormous pewter figurine collections who frequently sport jester hats and velvet capes who invite you to an all night star treck theme party.

Guys who try to hit on you with the aid of a dummy.

"Hi there, sexy lady!"

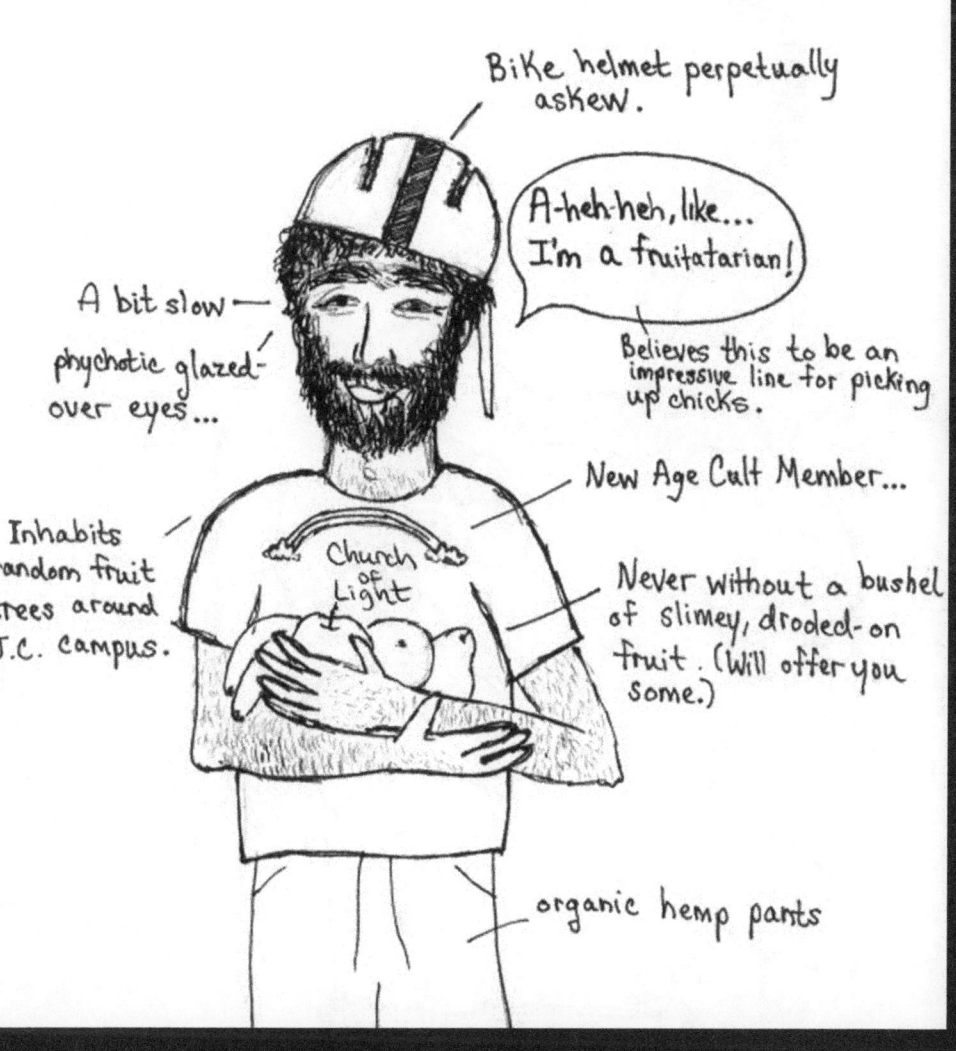

Dumb guys with dumb tatoos.

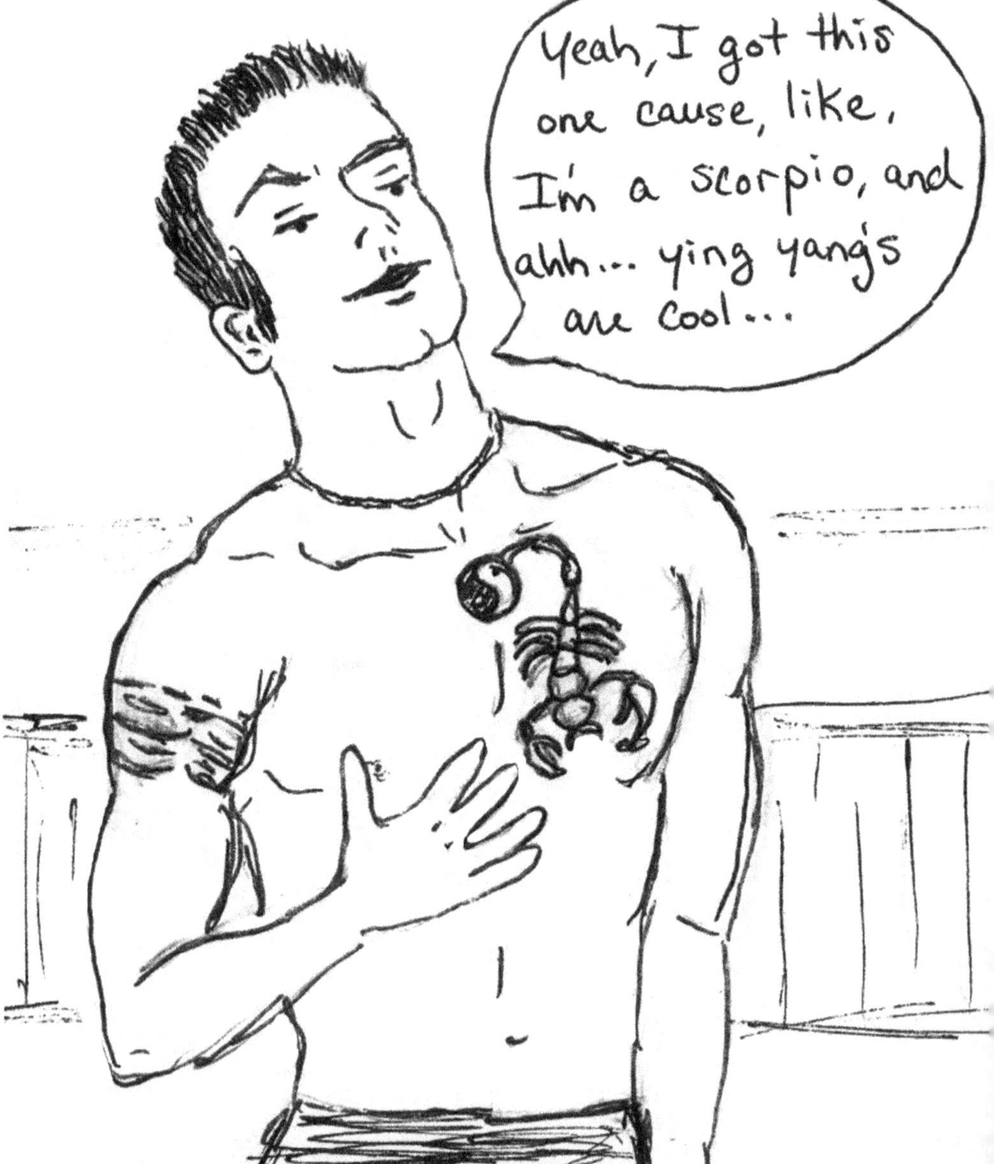

Really pretty guys...

Guys who like to dress up as clowns "for fun".

Bar dudes who can barely stay on their stool, yet still manage to bore a hole into your soul with their drunken eyes...

Guys on ecstasy who try to hug you.

"Hey, soul sister, I can feel some crazy vibrations flowing from your heart chakra to mine!"

Just Breathe

Guys who are only comfortable communicating with women online.

Smug, rich guys who try to impress you with their extensive wine collection and horrible paintings they purchased high on cocaine.

"Would you like to see my favorite piece of work? It's up in the master bedroom..."

Young Elite Magazine

Guys who hit on you, even though they've already found a couple of drunk chicks.

"Wanna board this train, baby?"

Young, sullen, guys who are obsessed with indie rock, their broken hearts, and their excessively fussed over hair.

Haunted, unkempt, Jesus look-alikes.

Scruffy groups of guys jamming in the Guerneville square, who are trying to recruit "chick singers".

# Summertime Hippy Festival Nomad

- **Long dreads secured under turban**
- **"Ren" fair accent**: "Sister, I am Eaglesaunce." (Self-given name discovered on vision quest)
- **Open heart chakra** (as well as a friendly lower chakra)
- **Raw silk vest** – nothing on underneath
- **Guatemalan Sarong-diaper**
- **Man-purse** containing crystals, raw nuts and seeds, homemade Kombucha in glass jar – will offer ladies a taste.
- **Jesus-style Sandals**

Sweaty yoga instructors with ponytails who hit on you after class...

*I think you may be ready to try the upward thrusting dog...*

www.ingramcontent.com/pod-product-compliance
Lightning Source LLC
Chambersburg PA
CBHW031211090426
42736CB00009B/876